Ife

MY
NAME
MEANS
LOVE

MY
NAME
MEANS
LOVE

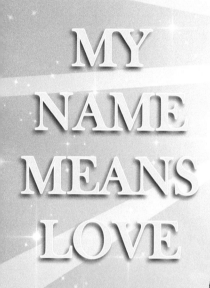
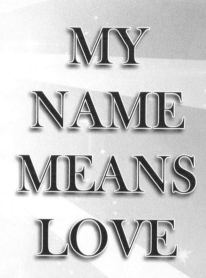

IFE: MY NAME MEANS LOVE
BY IFE J. T ALICTO

LOVE

LOVE

To order additional copies of this book, contact:
Xlibris
844-714-8691
www.Xlibris.com
Orders@Xlibris.com

ISBN: Softcover   978-1-6641-6733-9
       Hardcover   978-1-6641-7254-8
       EBook   978-1-6641-6732-2

Print information available on the last page

Rev. date: 05/06/2021

IFE: MY NAME MEANS LOVE
BY IFE J. T ALICTO

IFE: MY NAME MEANS LOVE

A long time ago in a land far, far, far away, there lived a girl named Ife! Ife, they called her; Ife was her name. The name originates from ancient Yoruba city in south-western Nigeria and meant "love."

When I was a child, my mom told me she had a dream that I came from the beach. She named me Ife, and a relative told my mother that she had an ancestor also named Ife. The name was given to me because my mom knew I had enough guts to handle it. Ife is a unique name, and so it should be treated as such. Mispronunciation of the name is not tolerated, and in order to talk to someone with this name you should learn how to say it first.

Migrating to America, I did not know I would change who I was to become who I am. Ife, my mother said as she walked into the cafeteria on a cloudy Wednesday afternoon, in her Trinidadian accent. Everyone looked around, trying to figure out whose name that was. Feeling embarrassed, I spoke up and said, "Mom, why are you not calling me Jumila?"

Jumila is my middle name. It is simple to say and easy to pronounce. Trinidadians would have loved my name, I thought to myself, but I did not want to be called Ife, a name that no one in New York could pronounce.

I had trouble pronouncing other people's names, I thought. How would I expect anyone and everyone to pronounce my name correctly. It's a shame how language is overlooked in the school system. When I came to America, I was about five years old. The year was 1987; I do not know the exact month. The education system in New York City in the late eighties and early nineties was very poor. Now that I am older, I am playing catch up. I admit I could have caught up years ago. Education is the foundation of life, in my opinion. Pronunciation is a skill we learn as children, and if I had known that, I would have stood up for myself when people did not pronounce my name correctly. I would have used my name in school and not shied away from it because I was ashamed. If I had known my roots and how powerful the name Ife is, I would have lived up to it.

Life took a turn in 1998. This is the year I learned that I was an immigrant. I knew I was not born in the United States, but I did not know I was an illegal alien. I had heard the term so many times growing up, but I just thought it was something people said to make fun of people who spoke differently. I did not know it was an actual label for people who were living illegally in the country. I also did not know all the things you have to do to become an American citizen. My dream of going to college and living on campus was shattered to little pieces that day. A girl can dream. We did not have money for college, so I do not know why I was so upset or how I was going to accomplish that dream. All I knew was that if I was American, it could happen.

My mom sat us down and said college was possible but that we all were illegal aliens. Our visas had expired and she didn't have the resources, meaning the money, to file the paperwork for us. My mother struggled; she had a rare sickness. Hearing what my mother told us, my sister and I looked at each other in disbelief. My sister was about to graduate high school and was excited about life. I was in la-la land as usual. My mother's biggest goal in life at that moment was for her two daughters to graduate high school. She was right; graduating high school for a black person is an accomplishment. If you can get through high school, you can succeed in higher education.

Being black in America sometimes feels like a crime. No matter how old I get or how many things I have accomplish, society lets me know that I am black and my life is not valued. I know this for sure. My mother, as I remember, said, "Society can take material things away from you, but they cannot take away your education." When my sister and I realized that we were immigrants, it became clear that in order to achieve the American dream of going to college with financial help from the government, we would need social security numbers. This was something we did not have; I had no idea what a social security number was at this time. I had no idea what this number would mean for my future goal of becoming a lawyer.

Becoming a lawyer was a dream of mine when I was younger. I loved to argue, I was confrontational and assertive, and so I thought I would be a good lawyer. Little did I know it requires a lot of reading comprehension, something I struggled with then and still do today. Now, as I think about my reaction, I understand I was being a terrible daughter; I did not know all the sacrifices my mom had to make. She gave up her life for me. She could have come to America with no children, but she decided to bring us to America in order for us to have a better life. I can only imagine how she felt moving to America and leaving the only country she had ever known to live in a big city with a sky-rocketing crime rate, with drugs and murder happening so constantly they became part of our everyday life.

The reality of my dreams for the future not turning out as I had planned was devastating. I wanted the dream sold to me on TV: the dream of going to college, living on campus, and partying with my friends. I wanted that dream so badly that I became lost in the thought. I became depressed. I could not see anything else but the dream, to the point that I missed the last few years of my mother's life. I had no idea my mom would leave me a few years later.

My mother was spontaneous. She loved life! We had everything we needed and wanted—I mean everything! I had a roof over my head, a bed to sleep on, and a room to call my own. I even used to post pictures on the wall, especially of the singer Tyrese. I had a big crush on him. I had a bicycle to ride; I had so much. My life was good. I would not have change it for anything. God picked the best person for me to come through. My dad was a man who loved calling us sweetheart and darling. I felt like the sweetest kid alive.

When I turned nineteen years old. My sister and my mother treated me to dinner and a movie. We saw *The Best Man*. I love that movie; it makes me think of our little family every time I watch it. This was also the year my stepmom took us to get our working papers. I remember being excited because I could finally work. I used to do odd jobs by helping people and they paid me for my services, but making money at an actual job was important. I would have a job with a paycheck and money to help our household. Later on in the same year, my mom took us to get our resident cards. This meant a lot as well; we were finally on our way to achieving the American dream: the dream of ownership, the dream of having a legacy in a country that we could now call our own.

My sister found a job and eventually finished college. I moved to Georgia, then joined the United States Navy. I completed my master's degree in healthcare while serving on sea duty in the navy.

One day, I woke up to a heavy feeling. When I feel like this, I reflect on my past—my childhood and my mother, who has been gone for over fifteen years. I think about the difficulties, the good and the bad and the gray areas. All I know is that, time does change people. I am now married with four kids. My mind examines the time when I was fourteen, when my mother and I helped my aunt move to Virginia. I always remember that day because it was my first time ever being inside of a big rig truck. I looked up to my aunt. She was the first woman that I knew, that knew how to drive and who had a car. Growing up in New York City, driving was not common. We did not drive; we had public transportation. Seeing her driving, I knew one day I would be doing the same.

My son TyTy loves trucks; it does not matter what kind. He will hit you over the head with a truck book if you do not read it to him. The Hertz truck was the biggest on the lot, and my cousin was the only one able to drive the big rig. My younger cousin and I were in the back seat of the minivan while my mother sat in the passenger seat. I felt my mother being worried about her nephew driving the truck; he was of age. Back then I wanted to be him someday—fearless and independent. Now I just want to be like my mom. She did not care what people thought about her; she lived her life and did not entertain the chatter. My little cousin who sat in the back seat with me was more like my mother's child—they both lived their lives for themselves, for no one else. My aunt moved to Virginia to be with her grandchildren and would go on one day to help me raise my first child. My older cousin was inspirational. Seeing a woman I knew in the military was exciting. That day at the age of fourteen was when I realized I had a dream to do something with my life.

In 2006, I started on this new journey. All I wanted to do was to get away from this old life and create a new one in a career that I once would never have dreamed of for myself. A career in the military required a completely new set of skills as well as dedication. Since my mother had passed away, I had nothing to lose. I had to learn that it was not always about me but often about a mission way bigger than myself. I had to learn how to incorporate a new set of values into my life.

Dedication to the mission was not for me. I did not understand, and I was very rebellious. I felt left out, and I did not know how to balance my past life with my new one. Everything just seemed so hard, but in 2009 when I picked up the rank of second-class petty officer in the navy, I started to see things a little differently. My first child, Ilias, was born, and it was not about me anymore. It was about who I represented as a woman, a mother, and an ambassador in the military. I worked with leadership who wanted to see me succeed. They trained me, and in turn I trained all of those who worked for me. I always spoke the truth about my struggle to balance a demanding life that I have since grown accustomed to. I loved the fact that, with time, life experience changes you. The people around me changed me, and I learned that new accomplishments were possible if I applied myself and never forgot where I came from, who I was, or how I got there.

I am in the military, and I have thrived. I believe this is because of God and all the people that helped me along the way. I am thankful God has positioned me in the right spaces to be successful. I remember sitting with the immigration lawyer to process our paperwork. I had no clue that this meant one day I would be living out a dream that my parents had for us. The day I became a citizen my son was released from the hospital. He was tiny, the year was 2010, and he was my date for my citizen ceremony. Now that I am in my thirties, I have a few more years to go. I am not rushing because as the days move forward, I get older. I feel excited to know God is not finished with me. My kids are the future. My mother struggled for the legacy I now uphold: to be educated, to treat people fairly, and to advocate for myself and for others. I look forward to seeing my immigrant story continue to grow. I wonder if my mom, an immigrant who worked hard to make sure we achieved the American dream, I always felt as if she was not done.

When I came to live in a new country, where I was judged for the color of my skin and for my name, I was embarrassed. I did not like my first name. I would say to myself, "Who would be able to pronounce a name that is spelled like this?"

People would say to me, "What a beautiful name!" I knew they were secretly saying, "How do you pronounce this unique name?"

My mother dreamt I came from the water; my ancestors were stolen from Africa and brought to Trinidad on a boat. This lets me know I am a queen. My name is love, and I stand fast. I realized three years ago as I researched my history that my mother gave me a name of love. I honor my name now and say it proudly! Ife: my name means love.

Acknowledgements

To my sons, Ilias and Tyberius, you bring joy, laughter, and hope into my life. If I did not have you, I do not know if I would have written a book about life in America. Thank you for being patient with me. Your mom is in the United States Navy, and I know it is a challenge.

To my daughters, Leona and Caitlyn, I am thankfully to your mother for allowing you to be part of my life. Thank you for your love.

To my husband, Jonathan, words cannot explain my love for you. You came into my life at a time when things were rough. God sent you for me; you came and found me. To my best friend, Chastity, who is always there to listen when all I want to do is vent. Thank you for investing your spiritual wisdom into our friendship. To my cousin Etta, thank you for showing me anything is possible. Thank you to my therapist at the time I was writing this book; without you I would have never realized that I have a story to tell in order to acknowledge my roots. Thank to my dad Carlton, who was part of giving me life and to my stepmom Maureen, for making sure we were good in this world. Thank you to my family. Thank you to my sister, Kizzy, I love you with all my heart you experienced this journey with me. We do not have the same story, but it is good to know I am not alone. To my mother, Cheryl Ann, when you passed away on October 16, 2004, you left as an immigrant to this land; you raised two daughters by yourself and you fought the great fight. Thank you, Mom, for teaching me our West Indian roots and for your words of wisdom, "Fame and fortune do not bring happiness."

Printed in the United States
by Baker & Taylor Publisher Services